Louisa May
ALCOTT

Author of LITTLE WOMEN

A CREATIVE ARTS BIOGRAPHY

Louisa May Alcott: Author of <u>Little Women</u>

BY ANNE COLVER
ILLUSTRATED BY CARY

ABOUT THE BOOK: This warm story of the life of Louisa May Alcott will be welcomed by young readers just as Miss Alcott's own books have delighted children for years. The author presents a clear picture of the character of Louisa herself and includes as well graphic portraits of the members of her family and others close to her on whose personalities Louisa based many characters in her books. This biography will make Miss Alcott's life and books more meaningful to young readers. This book is one of Garrard's *CREATIVE ARTS BIOGRAPHIES*, which tell the life stories of the truly creative geniuses of the world and provide hours of worthwhile pleasure reading.

Subject classification: Biography
Sub-classification: Authors, Reading

ABOUT THE AUTHOR: Anne Colver is the daughter of a newspaper reporter and began writing at the age of 12, when she and a friend "published" the WEEKLY BUGLE. She was graduated from Sidwell's Friends School in Washington, D. C., Pine Manor Junior College in Massachusetts, and Whitman College in Washington state. Her first book was a mystery novel; then she moved to biography and historical fiction. Now she specializes in books for young readers. In private life, Anne Colver is Mrs. Stewart Graff of Irvington, New York. She and her husband, also a writer, work on separate books, have collaborated on several, and have a son and daughter. Miss Colver has written some 27 books, including several for Garrard.

Reading Level: Grade 5
144 pages . . . 5¾ x 8¼

Interest Level: Grades 4–7
Publisher's Price: $2.49

Illustrated with photographs and line drawings; full-color lithographed cover; reinforced binding; index

GARRARD PUBLISHING COMPANY

Louisa May
ALCOTT
AUTHOR
OF *LITTLE WOMEN*

by Anne Colver

illustrated by Cary

GARRARD PUBLISHING COMPANY
Champaign, Illinois

To

Anne Louise Harris in the hope

that she will enjoy knowing Louisa

as much as her grandmother does

Picture Credits:

Alcott, Louisa May. *Flower Fables.* New York: McLoughlin Bros., 1854: p. 62
Alcott, Louisa May. *Little Men.* Boston: Roberts Bros., 1871: p. 123
Alcott, Louisa May. *Little Women.* Boston: Roberts Bros., 1868, 1869: p. 109
Alcott, Louisa May. *Louisa May Alcott: Life, Letters and Journals.*
    Boston: Roberts Bros., 1889: p. 114
Alcott, Louisa May. *Under the Lilacs.* Boston: Roberts Bros., 1878: p. 129
Bettmann Archive: p. 1, 2, 9, 16, 67, 84, 137
Concord Free Library: p. 45
Culver Pictures: p. 72, 79
Louisa May Alcott Memorial Association: p. 10, 13, 51, 54, 118, 139
Ticknor, Caroline. *May Alcott, a Memoir.* Boston: Little, Brown, 1928: p. 120, 132

Contents

1. "Look Out for Louisa..."

"Look out for Louisa! Here she comes!" A red-haired boy shouted the warning to a group of little girls in the Boston Common.

It was a spring morning in 1840. The sun was bright, and dandelions dotted the new green grass.

The girls jumped back just as seven-year-old Louisa May Alcott dashed past them, long legs flying, and stopped, breathless, beside her sister Anna. She had won a hoop-rolling race around the big park.

"Louisa always wins," one of the little girls sniffed. She smoothed her starched pinafore and looked down at her pantalettes and prim black slippers.

Louisa paid no attention. Her dress, like Anna's, was homemade of rough brown cloth. Her shoes were scuffed, and she had torn one stocking climbing a tree. She walked towards the red-haired boy, pushing back her long dark hair and laughing.

"Hooray, Louisa," he said. "Will you race me tomorrow?"

The hour chimed from a church near the Common. Noon recess was over. The boys and girls hurried back to their school. Louisa and her older sister walked in another direction to the small private school taught by their father, Bronson Alcott.

The girls remembered when Father had had a large, successful school in the Masonic Temple building. Mr. Alcott's ideas were different from those of other teachers of his time. He did not believe that children should simply memorize schoolbook lessons. He thought that they should be taught to study, ask questions, and learn to think for themselves. He never whipped boys for bad behavior as other teachers did. Instead he tried to teach them to *want* to be good.

At first many Boston parents had admired Mr. Alcott's new ideas and sent their children to his school. The children loved the way he taught and learned their lessons well. Then suddenly parents had begun to take their children away, and the Temple School failed.

A classroom in Mr. Alcott's Temple School.

Bronson Alcott was known as a scholar, teacher, philosopher, and dreamer.

Mrs. Alcott explained to Anna and Louisa: "Many people feel that Father's ideas are too modern and different, because he teaches children to study nature and to learn how people think and feel. He does not believe in copy books."

A few pupils had stayed in Mr. Alcott's school. He taught them and his daughters in his home.

It was nearly time for afternoon classes, as Louisa and Anna hurried through the narrow city streets. The sisters were a year and a half apart in age. Louisa's stormy nature and Anna's gentleness made them very different, but they were close companions. They called each other Nan and Lu.

Reaching home, Louisa flung open the front door. "Lu won the hoop-rolling race again," Nan called.

The house was strangely quiet. There was no answer from Mr. Alcott, no cheery greeting from their mother. The girls were puzzled. They peeked into the schoolroom. The pupils' chairs were empty. Their father was not at his desk.

Still more puzzled, the girls started upstairs. "Marmee," they called, using their favorite name for their mother. *"Marmee..."*

"Sh-sh," Mrs. Alcott beckoned from the landing. Four-year-old Beth, their youngest sister, held her mother's skirt. In a hushed voice Marmee told the girls that the children's parents had come to take Father's last pupils away because they learned he had taken a little Negro girl into the class. Now Father would have no school at all.

"Poor Father," Nan said, beginning to cry.

Louisa's face flushed with anger. "It isn't fair!" She stamped her foot.

Anxious weeks followed. Mr. Alcott could not find other work in Boston as a teacher. Their small amount of money was not enough for rent and food.

Mrs. Alcott's family lived in Boston. Her father, Colonel Joseph May, and her brothers offered to help. But the Alcotts were proud. "We will find our own way, God willing," Mr. Alcott said.

"Or even unwilling," his wife added. Even her brave spirit failed one evening when she had only rice to boil for the family supper. Still she set the table carefully with her best china and her few pieces of family silver. She put a scarlet geranium on the table. Mr. Alcott gave thanks for their food, and the others bowed their heads. When he had finished Louisa burst out angrily, "I hate boiled rice and I *won't* be thankful!"

There was a moment of silence. Then Mrs. Alcott said quietly, "If we can't be thankful, let us at least be cheerful." She served the plates

Cottage, Sunday, June 21st 1840.

My Dear Louisa

We all miss the noisy little girl who used to make house and garden, barn and field ring with her footsteps, and even the hens and chickens seem to miss her too. Right glad would Father and Mother, Anna and Elisabeth, and all the little mates at School, and Miss Russell, the House Play-room, Dolls, Hoop, Garden, Flowers, Fields, Woods and Brooks, all be to see and answer the voice and footsteps, the eye and hand, of their little companion. But yet all make themselves happy and beautiful

"Be good, little Miss, while away from us," her father wrote to eight-year-old Louisa who was visiting Grandfather May.

with a serene smile that made the poor meal seem less meager. Afterwards they sang together, and Father read out loud as usual.

The next morning's mail brought a surprise. Mr. Alcott had loyal friends among scholars and philosophers who still believed he was a gifted teacher. The letter was from Ralph Waldo Emerson, one of the most important lecturers and writers in America. Mr. Emerson had heard of the failure of Bronson Alcott's school. He wrote to tell them of a small cottage in Concord village where the Alcotts could live. It would cost little, he said, for the rent was cheap, and there was enough land for a vegetable garden to feed the family. Would they come? Mr. Emerson enclosed a check to help them pay for moving.

The Alcott family's spirits rose like bubbles. Mr. Alcott wrote to thank his good friend. Then he began to pack his books.

The three girls had gleeful visions of living in the country. "We'll have chickens and a cow and a horse and dogs, and a barn to play in!" Louisa clapped her hands.

2. "You Dasn't Dare..."

The Alcott family drove into Concord in a rickety old hired wagon that carried all their belongings.

Mr. Emerson, a tall thin man, clasped Father's hand warmly and said, "Here is your house." He led them to a shingled cottage that stood on an acre of land just off the road. Lilacs bloomed by the front door. The Concord River flowed lazily past the meadow's edge.

Mrs. Emerson greeted the newcomers with a basket of food for their first supper. "My children are having a lemonade tea in our barn," she told the girls. "Do come and join them."

Louisa and Nan ran off eagerly. As city children they had never dreamed of so much space to play in. They met the young Emersons—two boys and a little girl—and came home carrying three kittens.

The Alcotts moved to Concord in 1840 and made the pleasant New England village their own.

"Mrs. Emerson gave them to us," Louisa said. "Nan's is the striped one. Mine is black. The white one is for Beth."

By suppertime the Alcott house had a cozy, settled look. Father had chopped wood for the fire, and a kettle of soup bubbled in the kitchen.

Their old sofa stood beside the fireplace, its springs sagging comfortably. Father's books were on the shelves. Marmee's dining room table was polished, and her red geranium stood in the center. Father had staked out his vegetable garden and marked the fruit trees.

The next morning Louisa and Nan raced out to play. "We went wading in the river and hunted for frogs and made heaps of friends," Louisa told her mother. "I like the boys best. Cy Hosmer dared me to jump the brook. I did and I only got a little wet."

The Alcotts were soon on friendly terms with their Concord neighbors. Most of them were comfortable village families, but a few were different.

Mr. Alcott told them that young Henry Thoreau

was a distinguished naturalist. Mr. Thoreau took the Alcotts to visit Walden Pond nearby, where he had built a cabin and studied life in the woods. The girls were startled at first by Mr. Thoreau's gruff voice. But he introduced them to birds and frogs and chipmunks as though they were his friends and showed them how to walk softly and not disturb the wild creatures. Paddling silently, he pointed to fish that flicked along the lake bottom.

The story writer, Nathaniel Hawthorne, moved to Concord not long after the Alcotts did. Louisa often saw Mr. Hawthorne walking about the village. She thought his long cape and dark mustache made him look as romantic and mysterious as one of the characters in his books.

Mr. Alcott found work in Concord as a farm helper and as a carpenter. He had grown up on a farm and learned carpentering as a boy.

"It troubles me to see you doing this work," Mr. Emerson said, "when you should be recognized as a great teacher."

Louisa heard her father answer quietly,

"We are happy here and earn enough to feed ourselves. The rest will follow later."

In Concord the girls continued to study with their father. Even in the summer holiday they were expected to be up at five each morning for a cold shower. Before breakfast they read from the books Mr. Alcott gave them and wrote often in their journal diaries. Each helped with the housework. Bad manners were never allowed. Louisa and her sisters understood the family rules. But Louisa's quick temper sometimes led her into trouble.

One day she was rude to Marmee, and Father sent her to her room "to think about her bad behavior." After thinking for a while, she stole out and killed a spider. Then she buried him with a shingle for a tombstone and felt better.

The girls were always encouraged to play outdoors. Louisa still tagged after Cy Hosmer. They played crack-the-whip and Cy dared Louisa to be the "tail." When she fell and skinned her knees she heard Cy say, "She's a brave little thing. You can't make her cry."

After such praise Louisa was determined never to fail her hero.

The test came a few days later when Cy coaxed Louisa to climb to the highest beam in a neighborhood barn. Then he called, "You dasn't jump. I bet you dasn't dare!"

Louisa looked down dizzily. The hay-covered floor seemed miles below. But Cy had dared her. She shut her eyes and whispered, "One-two-three — *jump!*"

She landed with a crash and sprained both ankles. Carried home on a board, Louisa bore the pain gladly as Cy walked beside her.

Father shook his head. "Louisa's sprained ankles will keep her at home for at least a week," he said. "Perhaps that will teach her the difference between courage and foolishness."

After a few restless days indoors, Louisa thought of a new game. She lined up the Alcott family dolls and announced that Thomas Doll was accused of murder. All her friends were invited to poor Mr. Doll's trial.

Nan and Beth helped Louisa act out the story.

Louisa was the Judge. "Thomas Doll, you have been found guilty of murder," she said. "You are sentenced to death."

There was a piercing shriek from Nan, who spoke for the prisoner's wife. "No — no! Have mercy, please, your Honor. Do not make me a widow and leave this poor child without a father!" She pushed her younger sister forward.

Beth burst into tears.

"Well," said Judge Louisa, "I would pardon Mr. Doll, but our friends have already been invited to the funeral. Thomas Doll will have to be hung and buried. Then we can dig him up next week, and he can go back to his family."

The audience applauded loudly. Beth dried her tears.

The girls played other games. They loved to act out one of their favorite books, *Pilgrim's Progress*. It was the story of Christian's dangerous adventures as he traveled past the Giant Despair and through the Enchanted Ground to the happiness of the Celestial City. The girls borrowed Marmee's scrap bags to carry on their backs, and

"traveled" from the cellar to the "Celestial City" in the attic.

One midsummer dawn Mr. Alcott wakened his daughters. "You have a new baby sister," he told them, beaming. "Her name is May — for your grandfather, Colonel May."

Louisa exclaimed in quick disappointment, "Oh dear, I had prayed for a little brother!" But she welcomed the new baby as warmly as her family did.

Grandfather May and Marmee's brother, Uncle Samuel May, came from Boston for little May's christening. Louisa thought her white-haired grandfather looked even taller than she remembered. He still wore old-fashioned breeches and a cape.

When Uncle Samuel, who was a minister, sprinkled water on the baby's forehead to christen her, the others bowed their heads. Louisa stared at her grandfather's feet in huge, silver-buckled shoes.

Next morning Grandfather May perched Nan and Louisa on his knees for a lively game of

Simon-says-thumbs-up. When they made mistakes Grandfather's rumbling laugh was jolly. He saw that shy Beth did not join in the games. Later he took Beth and her kitten in his lap and told a quiet story.

Grandfather patted each girl's head when he said good-bye. "Mind you be good," he said to Louisa. "When you come to visit, you shall ride the gray pony your mother used to ride."

"I wish I *would* be good," Louisa sighed later to Marmee. She still struggled with her temper. Nan's diary pages were about happy events, but Louisa's were often full of worries. Once she wrote, "I am so cross I wish I had never been born . . . I cried when I went to bed and made good resolutions. If I only kept all I make I should be the best girl in the world. But I don't and so am very bad."

Christmas came and the meadows were drifted high with snow. Mr. Alcott cut pine branches to fill the house with their spicy smell.

Louisa was the first one awake in the chilly Christmas dawn. She tiptoed downstairs to put

her presents in the stockings hanging by the fireplace. She had made penwipers for Father, a potholder for Marmee, a hair bow for Nan and a knitted scarf full of dropped stitches for Beth. Marmee had helped her make a rag doll for baby May.

Later the Alcotts gathered before the fire to roast chestnuts and sing their favorite carols as they opened presents. The gifts were homemade and simple, but each held a special gift of love.

They ate dinner at the Emersons' and walked home together over the crunching snow. Marmee held Beth's hand. Father carried the baby May. Nan and Louisa ran ahead. Louisa stopped and patted her stomach, full of plum pudding.

"I wish every day could be Christmas," she said. "Then I would always be good."

3. "I Ran in the Wind and Played Be a Horse..."

With the new baby to care for, Mrs. Alcott had less time to read and play with the older girls. Nan was often busy helping her mother.

Louisa had always loved books. Now she spent more time reading. One rainy afternoon she curled up on the sofa with an exciting chapter from a new book, when a small sigh made her look up. Six-year-old Beth sat by the hearth with her doll Joanna in her lap. Poor Joanna, bedraggled and half bald, was tender-hearted Beth's special favorite.

Beth must feel lonely sometimes, Louisa thought suddenly. She is too shy to make friends and too patient and good to complain. Louisa put her exciting chapter aside. "Bethy, would you like me to make a new dress and bonnet for Joanna?" she asked.

"Oh, could you, Lu?" Beth's wistful face brightened. "Joanna would love to be pretty again."

Louisa borrowed Marmee's piece bag and spilled out bright scraps of cloth and ribbons. In spite of her tomboy ways, Louisa had learned to sew from Marmee and was clever at it. While she snipped and stitched, Louisa told Beth a story of a beggar girl named Joanna, who dreamed she had a new dress and a bonnet with purple ribbons. "When she woke up the dream had come true — and here she is!" Louisa held up Joanna.

Beth brought Joanna in her new finery to the supper table. "Lu did it," she said proudly.

Another year went by in Concord. On long summer days the girls went wading and rowed on the river. The Alcotts took picnic suppers into the woods, and Mr. Alcott read aloud from the Charles Dickens novels which were their favorite books. Louisa listened breathlessly to the adventures of *Oliver Twist*. As twilight fell and the story grew more exciting, the girls begged, "Just one more chapter, please?" *Pickwick Papers* was another favorite Dickens book.

The next spring a change broke the happy family circle. Mr. Alcott was asked to lecture in England about his ideas of teaching children.

It took all of the family savings, with help from Mr. Emerson, to pay for Mr. Alcott's journey. The girls were lonely without him, but Mrs. Alcott said, "This is a great honor for Father. His ideas about teaching have never been understood in this country. Surely the people in England will appreciate him."

Letters from Mr. Alcott told of his success. Distinguished audiences came to hear him lecture.

On a happy day in August, Father returned home. Louisa and Nan and Beth raced to welcome him. Baby May toddled after them calling, "Far-vee, Far-vee!"

The joy of welcome was soon cooled. Mr. Alcott had brought friends from England. Mr. Charles Lane was a thin, sober-looking man. His son William, just a year older than Nan, was as unsmiling as his father.

Mrs. Alcott welcomed the guests hospitably but Louisa grumbled, "Mr. Lane interrupts our lessons with Father. He never likes us to laugh. And William is a crosspatch!"

"I wish they'd go home," Nan sighed.

Far from going home, Charles Lane shared a great plan with Mr. Alcott. They would start a new society where people would live together in harmony and peace and not work for money but only to help each other. The men found a rambling old farm near the village of Harvard, halfway to Boston, and planned to move there. They called the new settlement *Fruitlands*.

"We will have no money," Mr. Alcott explained

serenely, "but will live only on the bounty of nature. Fruit and berries and vegetables and grain from our fields will feed us."

Mrs. Alcott listened sympathetically. She believed in her husband's high ideals. She sewed the plain linen robes they all would wear. Still, she wondered who would pay for cloth and needles and thread at *Fruitlands.*

The Alcotts and the Lanes moved to their new home on the first day of June, 1842. Louisa sat on a high wagon seat beside Father. She and

Nan waved a sad farewell to their Concord friends. Beth wept bitterly because her precious cats must be left behind. Cats made Mr. Lane sneeze.

In spite of missing her playmates, Louisa's first weeks at *Fruitlands* were happy. She loved the wide fields and the woods. It was fun to climb the orchard trees and help pick apples and cherries.

"I ran in the wind and played be a horse," Louisa wrote in her journal.

With fruit and wild berries, fresh vegetables, and honey, there was plenty to eat during the summer. A stream of visitors came to observe the new experiment at *Fruitlands*. Some, like Mr. Emerson and the Reverend Theodore Parker, admired the noble plan of living. "They look well in July. We will see them in December," Mr. Emerson wrote.

The rosy dream that other families would join the settlement soon faded. Most visitors came only to "see the queer people at *Fruitlands*." Few stayed long, or helped work in the fields or in the house. Cooking, scrubbing, and sewing were left to Mrs. Alcott, with the girls to help. Even small May learned to fill her tin pail with currants or raspberries.

When school began, William Lane and the Alcott girls were the only pupils. Mr. Lane shared the teaching with Mr. Alcott and was more strict. Louisa fidgeted under Mr. Lane's stern eye and scowled over the rules of grammar he made them learn. She hated rules, preferring to write from free imagination. But he taught

Louisa a style and discipline she never forgot.

Cold weather came and the old farmhouse was drafty. It was a rule at *Fruitlands* that they must not wear wool or leather clothes, since animals must not be used to serve man. On chilly days they shivered, with only thin linen robes and cloth sandals to wear. No meat must be eaten and, without fruit and vegetables from the garden, the meals became a dreary round of potato soup and mush with dried apples.

One night after a supper of boiled parsnips, which Louisa detested, she went to bed in the big attic room the three older girls shared. Louisa was too hungry to sleep. Suddenly she said, "Let's imagine we're eating our favorite foods. I'm eating chicken with dumplings and gravy and caramel pie."

Nan and Beth chimed in. "I'm eating strawberry shortcake . . ." "Pancakes and syrup . . ." "Chocolate marshmallow cake . . ."

Louisa rolled over with a groan. "Stop! I'm too full to eat another bite!"

Family evenings were no longer happy times

when the family read aloud together. Mr. Lane chose dull, preachy books to read. Louisa listened, swallowing yawns, and remembered the happy times when Father had read in his rich, dramatic voice, and they had laughed and cried over *The Old Curiosity Shop* and other Dickens favorites.

Longing for excitement, Louisa and Nan made up plays and acted in them. Marmee helped with costumes. But Mr. Lane disapproved of such frivolous pastimes. Louisa grumbled, "It's no fun to act without an audience."

Soon afterward Louisa discovered an audience of her own. Late one night Mrs. Alcott heard strange thumps and muffled shrieks from the attic bedroom. She went to investigate and found Nan and Beth clinging together terrified while Louisa, wrapped in a sheet, crept toward them, whispering hoarsely that she was a mummy buried for 2000 years and just dug up.

The next day Mrs. Alcott suggested a new outlet for her daughter's alarming fancies. She gave Louisa and Nan blank notebooks.

"Call them 'imagination books,'" she said. "Write about anything you think of."

Both girls enjoyed the new writing. Nan's stories of captive maidens rescued by handsome princes had happy, romantic endings. Louisa's pages were scribbled with adventures in haunted castles, or bold thieves in search of pirates' gold. Her heroes dashed about on horseback and fought gory duels. But she no longer frightened her sisters at night with tales of ghosts and mummies.

4. "Now I Have a Room to Scribble In..."

Not even Mr. Lane's long face could dampen all the Alcott family fun. They trimmed a tree with popcorn and cranberries for their first Christmas at *Fruitlands*. Birthdays were celebrated with happy ceremony. A four-leaf clover or a loving note could be a gift. For Marmee's birthday the following October, Louisa "made her a moss cross and wrote a piece of poetry and promised to be good all day."

Louisa and her father shared the same birthday, November 29. Louisa was eleven that

November, 1843, as their second winter at *Fruitlands* began. Early frost had killed the crops. No more visitors came. The lonely little group had scarcely enough food for the cold months ahead.

Quarreling began. Mr. Lane said that if Mrs. Alcott and the girls left, the settlement might succeed. Mr. Alcott never considered asking his family to leave. But echoes of the quarrel upset Louisa and her sisters. They could not bear to think of the family being separated.

Louisa realized that her father and mother were unhappy and worried. "Father is unhappy and Mother worries," she wrote in her journal: "Nan and I cried in bed, and I prayed God to keep us all together."

One December afternoon Mr. Lane and his son William left *Fruitlands*. Louisa and Nan watched them drive away and hugged each other in relief.

Now the Alcott family was alone. But there were still worries. Mr. Alcott was ill with grief because his dream of a settlement living in harmony and peace had failed. Mrs. Alcott was exhausted by the months of work. Yet she took care of her husband tenderly, with never a reproach. Louisa and her sisters learned a lesson in loyalty and love.

The Alcotts could not take care of the big farm alone. Now Mrs. Alcott took charge. She sold some of her family silver and rented rooms from a family named Lovejoy in the nearby village of Still River. Grandfather May sent money to help the family move.

In the new home troubles faded gradually. Mr. Alcott grew stronger and found work plowing fields and cutting wood for his neighbors. Mrs. Alcott earned extra money sewing for Mrs. Lovejoy and her friends.

Louisa and her sisters went to the village school. By the end of the term each of the girls had a best friend to bring home after school.

A new friend came unexpectedly. One afternoon in June Mrs. Alcott returned from a trip to visit her family in Boston and brought home a lad she had met on the stagecoach. His name was Frederick Llewelyn Willis. His parents were dead, and he was on his way to live with elderly relatives for the summer.

When Fred met the Alcott family he wanted to stay with them. His guardian gave him permission to board for the summer.

Louisa decided Fred should be her special friend. She had always wanted a brother. At first she was disappointed. Fred was too shy to join in their play. The more Louisa coaxed him, the more he hung back from their games. One day Louisa teased him, "Come and play, come and play, or else go away and stay!"

That evening Beth slipped her small hand into Fred's. "Don't worry about feeling shy," she whispered. "I always do. When Louisa teases she likes to be teased back."

The next morning Fred stalked to his place at the breakfast table and put a large cardboard before his face. He had printed on the sign: "DO NOT SPEAK TO ME. I AM LOUISA." He proceeded to give an imitation of Louisa in one of her cross moods that convulsed the family. Then,

after one astonished moment, Louisa burst out laughing herself.

"Just wait, Fred Willis, I'll get even," Louisa said. "If you can act so well, you'll be in our next play. And no more excuses about being shy!"

After that day Fred learned to be part of the family. He joined in plays and pranks like any brother with four lively sisters. Whenever Louisa was too bossy Fred made a solemn face and said to her, "Do not speak to me." Louisa always laughed.

Fred helped Mr. Alcott in the garden and carried firewood for Mrs. Alcott. He and the girls went on picnics in the woods. Fred helped them find frogs and butterflies. When he laughed at Louisa for being afraid of spiders, she collected a jarful to show him how brave she was.

By the end of summer the thin, anxious look was gone from Fred's face. He was as tanned and cheerful as any Alcott. When he went back to school, his guardian promised that Fred could spend vacations with his "Alcott family."

The next year there were new plans for the Alcott family. Mrs. Alcott's father, Grandfather May, had died. With the money Marmee inherited from him, the Alcotts bought *Hillside*, an old brown shingled farmhouse in Concord, and the family moved once more.

The girls raced from the attic to the barn of *Hillside*. It was the first house the Alcott family had owned. "We'll never have to move again," Louisa said.

The girls came home after a first joyful tour of their old neighborhood. Beth brought a tiger kitten. One of the cats she had left behind was its mother.

"Just think, I'm a kitten grandmother," Beth said proudly.

One day Louisa and her mother met a friend in the village. "Dear me, can this tall young lady be Louisa?" the friend exclaimed. "Your little girls are growing into little women, Abba."

Louisa was almost thirteen but she did not like the idea of growing up. "Nan puts her hair up and talks about boys with the other girls but

Father made a sketch of *Hillside*, the Alcotts' happiest home.

I *won't*," Louisa told her mother. She added mournfully, "Everything has changed since we came back to Concord. Cy hasn't dared me to do a single thing."

One great joy came to Louisa when they moved into *Hillside*. Mr. Alcott had rebuilt the old farmhouse and added an extra wing on the ground floor. Louisa and Nan each had bedrooms of their own. Fourteen-year-old Nan sewed frilly curtains and a ruffled spread, but Louisa kept

her room plain. Blue skies outside her windows made the curtains. She could open her door to a meadow carpeted in summer green or winter white, and run as often as she liked. She had a desk and chair where she could write.

"Now that I have a room of my own to scribble in, I'll be happy," Louisa said.

Much of Louisa's scribbling went into plays which the girls acted in the Alcott barn. Louisa and Nan took most of the parts. They learned to change costumes quickly between scenes. Louisa had a pair of russet leather boots and loved to stomp around the stage as a villain. When Fred Willis came to board for summer vacations, he joined in the plays and family picnics.

The girls also had a literary society, the Pickwick Club, and met in the attic to read their poems and stories. "You can join us," Louisa told Fred, "but only if you write a story."

The summer Louisa was fourteen she went to visit her uncle's family in New Hampshire. She wrote to Nan about a boy named Augustus she met there. "He has blue eyes and a beautiful nose," Louisa wrote home to Nan. "He invited me to a huckleberry party and told me he thought chestnut hair the loveliest in the world."

Nan wrote back sympathetically. But Louisa was not ready to be sentimental. Even with her longer skirts, she still loved to climb trees and could vault a fence like a boy. When she came back to Concord, Augustus was almost forgotten.

Louisa found new problems at home. Nan whispered to her, "Father tries everywhere but he can't find enough work. If we have to move again, where will we go?"

Winter came. The neighbors knew the Alcotts did not have enough food. They left hampers of bread and jugs of milk on the doorstep. The Emersons sent eggs and butter. Mr. Thoreau brought dried corn and hickory nuts.

One morning Mrs. Alcott opened the door and found a basket of old clothes. A strange expression crossed her face. Then she held up a patched linen shirt.

"This will make a good play dress for May," she said. "I can shorten this skirt for Lu."

Louisa stamped her foot. "That skirt belonged to Minna Scott," she said. "I *won't* wear other people's old clothes!"

Mrs. Alcott said quietly, "Everything in this world passes from one person to another. It's no different to use another person's clothes than to read his books or enjoy his music."

It was a lesson for Louisa in the difference between false pride and honest pride. Marmee's clever fingers cut and turned and trimmed the

Order of In-door Duties
for Children.

Morning	Forenoon		Noon	Afternoon	Evening
5. Rise, Bathe, Dress.	9. Studies		1. Rest.	6. Supper.
6. Breakfast	with Mr Lane.		2. Sewing, Conversation,	Recreation.
Housewifery	10½ Recreations.	12 Dinner	and Reading with	Conversation.
Recreations.	11. Studies		Mother and Miss Foord.	Music.
(Chores) in care of	with		4. Errands and	8.
Miss Foord	Father		(Chores) Recreations.	8½ Bed.

Bathing Hours 5. 10½ 6.	Vigilance, Punctuality, Perseverance.	**Labor Hours** 6½ to 8. 2 to 4.
	Prompt, Cheerful, Unquestioning, Obedience.	**Play Hours** 8 to 9. 10 & 10½. 4 to 6
Study Hours 9 to 10½. 11 to 12.	Government of Temper, Hands, and Tongue.	**Eating Hours** 6 to 6½. 12 & 12½. 6 to 6½.
	Gentle Manners, Motions, and words.	**Sleeping Hours** 8 to 5. 8½ to 5.
	Work, Studies, and Play distinct.	
	No interchange of Labors.	

Observe Silence and Stillness.

Father's daily plan for his daughters. Louisa did not always observe "silence and stillness."

worn-out coats and dresses and bonnets to look like new. But Louisa, with her fiercely independent nature, longed for a time when she need not depend on favors from other people.

The Alcotts struggled through another year. Nan had the highest record for spelling and reading in school. Louisa won a prize for writing the best story. When summer came Nan and Louisa earned money teaching nature classes for younger children. Ellen Emerson was one of their pupils.

Louisa wrote stories for Ellen and the other children, called "Flower Fables." The simple fairy tales were very different from the wild adventure tales Louisa had written before. Mr. Emerson read the "Fables." "They are nicely written with real imagination," he said.

One afternoon Louisa came home to find Marmee in tears. She could not remember ever seeing her mother cry.

"A friend has offered me work in Boston if we will move there," Mrs. Alcott told Louisa. "It means giving up our home here. But Father can't find enough work in Concord. If we stay, we must live on charity. Oh, Lu, I can tell you these things because you seem to understand best."

Louisa put her arms around her mother. "Of course we'll go. It will be all right, Marmee. I promise." As she spoke, Louisa said good-bye to the dream of never having to move again. It faded like other Alcott dreams.

The four years at *Hillside* had been the happiest Louisa and her sisters had known. But in that moment Louisa knew their carefree times were ended. A sudden weight settled on her young shoulders. Somehow, in the cloudy future, she would rescue the family from disappointed dreams. "The Alcotts won't always be poor," she told herself fiercely.

The Alcotts moved from Concord on a bleak November day in 1849.

It was Louisa's birthday month. She would be sixteen.

5. "Now, Lu, the Door Is Open..."

The dark, narrow house the Alcotts rented in Boston was on Temple Street. There were no trees or meadows around them, only crowded city streets. But Alcott spirits were never discouraged for long. The house was settled quickly and their new life began.

Mrs. Alcott's work was as a "visitor to the poor." She was hired by a charity society to help immigrants who came from Europe to find work in America. She was filled with pity for

The Alcott girls' beloved "Marmee."

the distressed, bewildered families she met. "They are strangers without homes or friends," Mrs. Alcott told her family.

Louisa heard Marmee's stories. "I've complained of our being poor," she told Nan, "but we always had food and a warm house and our own beds. I didn't know we were really rich!"

Before long Mr. Alcott found new work. He gave lectures, called "conversations." He earned only a few dollars, but many philosophers and scholars came to hear him. Later he went on a lecture tour through the western states, hoping to earn more money. Louisa described the night he returned in her journal.

"In February Father came home. . . . A dramatic scene when he arrived in the night. We were waked by hearing the bell. Mother flew down, crying *'My husband!'* We rushed after, and five white figures embraced the half-frozen wanderer who came in hungry, tired, cold, and disappointed, but smiling bravely and as serene as ever. We fed and warmed and brooded over him . . . May said . . . 'Well, did people pay you?' Then, with a queer look, he opened his pocket-book and showed one dollar, saying with a smile that made our eyes fill, 'Only that! My overcoat was stolen and I had to buy a shawl. Many promises were not kept, and travelling is costly; but I have opened the way, and another year shall do better.'

"I shall never forget how beautifully Mother answered him, though the dear, hopeful soul had built much on his success; but with a beaming face she kissed him, saying, 'I call that doing *very well*. Since you are safely home, dear, we don't ask anything more.'"

Eight-year-old May went to school in Boston. Beth, the little homebody, "cooked and house-kept" while Marmee worked. Nan and Louisa earned money by opening a small school in the Alcott parlor. "Nan has Father's gift for teaching, but I haven't," Louisa confessed. "I hate pounding wisdom into unwilling little heads. But I keep pounding, and try to learn patience . . . like a proper schoolmarm."

Most young girls in Boston went to society balls and dances. "Nan and I are invited but can't go as we have no party dresses," Louisa wrote her Uncle Samuel. "I don't miss the frills and feathers, but Nan would love them."

Amateur theatricals were more to Louisa's liking. She and Nan still loved acting, and they joined a Boston dramatic club. Nan took romantic parts in the plays. One week Louisa was a tragic Hamlet. Another time she played the part of Sary Gamp, a comic old nurse from one of the Dickens novels, and set the audience laughing.

Fred Willis was now a student at Harvard College and came to see the Alcotts often. He had long ago outgrown his shyness. But he had not forgotten the love of fun and mischief he had learned from the Alcotts. Fred and Louisa joked and teased in the old way, while Beth and May sighed quite sentimentally over their handsome "brother."

One rainy evening Louisa lay stretched before the fire reading an exciting chapter of *The Count of Monte Cristo*. Suddenly Nan called from the window, "Here comes Marmee bringing a man and a woman and four—six, good heavens—*seven* children. And a baby! All of them needing supper, I'm sure!"

The unexpected guests were an immigrant

family just arrived from Germany. Marmee explained that her charity office could not find them a home until Monday. Meanwhile the Alcotts would make the strangers welcome.

The wet, shivering family, not understanding English, nodded gratefully and edged closer to the fire. Mrs. Alcott brought blankets and dry clothes, while Nan and Louisa hurried to the kitchen. They sliced bread, made porridge for the children, and put on an extra pot of coffee. Louisa poured water into the supper stew. "It's lucky Marmee taught us that thin soup and cheerful conversation can feed multitudes," she said.

"Our poor little home had much love and happiness in it, and was a shelter for lost girls, abused wives, friendless children, and weak or wicked men," Louisa wrote later in her journal. "Father and Mother have no money to give but give time, sympathy, help; and if blessings would make them rich, they would be millionaires!"

The Alcotts caught smallpox from one immigrant family. The girls had it lightly, but Father and Marmee were very ill.

After her recovery Mrs. Alcott was not strong enough to go back to the charity office. For a time she ran an agency finding work for women. Later the family moved to a larger house on Pinckney Street, where Marmee rented out the extra rooms. One of their first boarders was Fred Willis. He brought other Harvard students to the Alcotts', and the hungry lads did full justice to Marmee's best cooking.

One evening Fred and Louisa talked late. They were both in a serious mood. "Don't you write any more, Lu?" Fred asked. "You used to produce at least one masterpiece a week, and Marmee was convinced you would be a second Shakespeare."

Louisa shrugged. "I'm twenty-two now. I gave up scribbling along with other childish fun. Nan and I still long to go on the stage and lead gay lives. But we have our livings to earn—so we must give up dreams and grub along teaching." She turned to stare into the fire.

Fred studied Louisa's profile and was troubled. The other sisters had found their ways of expressing themselves. Nan loved teaching. Beth was contented at home. May sketched and painted with artistic ambition. Only Louisa had not found her path.

The next week, on an impulse, Fred opened an old trunk and took out a crumpled manuscript. It was an adventure story Louisa had written when the Alcotts lived in Concord. He copied the story carefully and took it to a newspaper editor who promptly bought it for five dollars.

Flower Fables

by
Louisa May Alcott

Decorations
by
Frances Bassett Comstock

McLoughlin Bros.
New York

A copy of Louisa's "first-born" book, "Flower
Fables," was in Marmee's Christmas stocking.

That evening Fred burst into the Alcott dining room, waving the check, and announced, "Louisa is an authoress!"

Louisa was astounded. First she hugged Fred. Then she scolded him, then burst into tears.

Louisa had never thought of her writing as a way to earn money. Now she set up a desk in the attic and wrote furiously in her spare time. Her next stories sold to the same editor for five dollars each. She recopied the "Flower Fables" she had written for Ellen Emerson and sold them as a book. She stuffed the first copy into Marmee's Christmas stocking, and the family hailed her success.

The little volume earned only thirty-two dollars for Louisa. But Uncle Samuel May wrote approvingly, "Now, Lu, the door is open—go in and win." Louisa wrote:

> ". . . people began to think that topsey-turvey Louisa would amount to something after all . . . Perhaps she may."

6. "Which Star I'll Hitch My Wagon To..."

In the spring of 1855 Louisa burst into Nan's room with good news. "A letter just came," she said. "Mother's New Hampshire cousins want us to come and live in a cottage they own in Walpole Village — *rent free* — for as long as we like. Marmee will have a snug home and rest from boarding house cares. Father can farm between lecture trips, and we shall all breathe fresh country air. What a lark after six years of city living!"

The summer months in Walpole were the most carefree the Alcotts had known since Concord days. Mr. Alcott's winter lectures had been successful. For the summer he planted crops and worked the fresh earth, "looking as serene and wise as Plato," Louisa said. Marmee and Nan sewed through the long afternoons. Beth took in homeless kittens from miles around, and May ecstatically sketched the mountain landscape.

Louisa kicked up her heels like a colt set free. After an early morning run, she said to Marmee, "In the city I'd begun to feel like an old lady of twenty-two. Now I'm young again!"

On rainy days Louisa went to the attic to work.

> "I am in the garret with my papers round me, and a pile of apples to eat while I write my journal, plan stories, and enjoy the patter of rain on the roof, in peace and quiet."

She sent a story, "King Goldenrod," to a Boston editor who promptly bought it.

Looking about for a new idea, Louisa noticed some of May's pen and ink sketches. "I'll write a book and you can illustrate it," Louisa said. Fourteen-year-old May was delighted. The two sisters worked together and produced a small book called *Christmas Elves*. Mr. Alcott looked over the manuscript. "Bless me, we've hatched *two* clever chicks," he told Marmee.

The family went for picnics in the green hills and read aloud together. Nan and Louisa acted in village plays, and were as stage-struck as ever. "I'll write the great American drama, and Nan shall be the star," Louisa promised. "May can design the scenery, and we'll be the famous Alcott sisters!"

Autumn came and the carefree summer ended. Nan went to teach in Syracuse where Uncle Samuel now lived. May started school in Walpole.

Louisa was restless. One day she talked to Beth. "If I'm to earn money, I must go back to Boston," she said. "But I don't like to leave you and May the only ones at home."

Louisa went off to Boston determined to become a famous author.

Beth patted Louisa's hand. "You go and be famous, Lu. May and the kittens and I will keep Father and Mother cheerful."

Louisa left one November day and wrote in her journal: "Decided to seek my fortune; so with my little trunk of homemade clothes, $20 earned by stories, and my manuscripts, I set forth . . ."

In Boston Louisa lived first with cousins. They were kind, but Louisa wanted more independence. She went to board with Mrs. Reed, an old family friend in Pinckney Street, and rented an attic room for three dollars a week. "There is only a skylight for a window, so I call it my sky parlor," Louisa wrote to Nan. "The sun blazes down all day. At night I watch the sky and wonder which star I'll hitch my wagon to."

Louisa found work as governess and teacher to a little invalid girl in Boston. In her spare time she sewed for Mrs. Reed and her friends. "I shan't get rich teaching or sewing," Louisa said, "but I can plan stories while I stitch and scribble 'em down on Sundays."

"I go to concerts and theater whenever I can afford to buy a ticket," Louisa wrote home. "Mrs. Reed is shocked at a young lady going about alone in this wicked city. 'What would your dear mother say?' she asks. I assure her that my dear mother has always known I was born with a boy's spirit under my bib and tucker!"

True to her promise Louisa wrote a play. She called it *Prima Donnas*. A Boston theater manager liked it, but after much delay the play was not produced. The manager gave Louisa a season pass for free theater tickets as consolation. She promptly forgot her disappointment, danced a jig for joy, and invited Fred Willis to the next performance. Fred was a frequent caller. "You keep me from being lonesome," Louisa told him. "You and I are 'Alcotts together.'"

Editors bought Louisa's stories as fast as she could write them. Now they paid ten or fifteen dollars, as her name was better known. She was grateful for the money and sent most of it home to buy extra comforts for the family in Walpole. Still, she was not satisfied to go on writing little tales of fantasy like "King Goldenrod" and "Flower Fables."

"I'm tired of elves and flowers and fairy princesses," Louisa told her father. "I want to write about real people and their joys and trials in a real world. But when I try, the words just won't come."

Mr. Alcott answered, "You must live before you can write about life. And you must work. You have real talent, Lu. It will grow naturally if you keep living and working."

When the Alcotts gathered for another summer in Walpole, Louisa's heart filled with alarm. Beth was ill with scarlet fever. Louisa nursed her tenderly, but Beth was very weak.

Beth's twenty-first birthday came in June. Nan was home on vacation. Marmee baked a cake, and Father made a birdhouse to hang on a branch outside Beth's window. Louisa and Nan gave her a lacy scarf and pretty new slippers. May had copied Beth's favorite songs and decorated the pages with watercolors. Louisa gave her comical imitation of Dickens' Sary Gamp.

When Beth said good night she smiled. "I'll get well now that we are all together and Lu can make me laugh."

Beth seemed stronger during the summer. But before Louisa went back to Boston, she whispered to Marmee, "If Beth is worse again, write me and I'll come."

Months passed. Louisa and May were both in Boston. May lived with an aunt and studied art with the distinguished Professor Rimmer. Louisa kept a sisterly eye on her youngest sister. "Professor Rimmer says May has real talent," Louisa wrote home. "Aunt gives May French lessons, and she spouts *parlez-vous* like a regular duchess. She was invited to her first ball, and I made her a white satin dress with blue velvet ribbons. Our pretty May loves society, and I shan't let her play second fiddle to any society flibbertigibbet."

That spring, word came from Marmee that Beth was weaker. Louisa went home to help. The Alcotts moved back to Concord in the autumn, hoping that Beth would be better there.

The wandering Alcotts settled at last in tree-shaded old *Orchard House.*

They bought another home, *Orchard House*, a gray shingled farmhouse near their old home, *Hillside*, now owned by the Hawthornes.

While Mr. Alcott made repairs on the old house, they lived in rented rooms in Concord. The girls all helped Marmee watch over Beth. Louisa took her share of the nursing at night. Beth asked her to play Sary Gamp to help pass the long hours when she could not sleep. "She tries to be gay that I may keep up," Louisa wrote in her journal. "Dear little saint! I shall be better all my life for these sad hours with her."

With each day Beth's spirit faded. One morning she called the family around her. "All here," she smiled. She gave away her few possessions and died a few days later, as gently as she had lived.

"So the first break comes," Louisa wrote.

Shy Beth never knew how many friends she had made. They crowded the church to attend the funeral service. Fred Willis came from Boston. Mr. Emerson and Mr. Thoreau stood with bowed heads.

Louisa and Nan stayed in Concord to help settle the new family home. Mr. Alcott had made the old house bright and comfortable.

"Much company to see the new house," Louisa wrote in her journal. "All seem to be glad that the wandering family is anchored at last. We won't move again for twenty years if I can help it!"

Another family change came later in the spring with Nan's engagement to John Pratt, a young teacher. The two families were old friends. John's father had been a visitor at *Fruitlands*.

Earlier in the year Nan and John had acted in a sentimental play together. Quiet John had never been a fiery actor. But he gazed into Nan's eyes and spoke his lover's lines so adoringly that the audience felt they were watching a true romance. "John and I were in love before the curtain came down," Nan confessed later to Louisa.

The Alcotts welcomed John as a new son and brother. Louisa said, "They moon about and sigh like a pair of tragic furnaces and then declare they are the two happiest people in the world!" She shook her head over the mysteries of love.

With all the family activity to keep her in Concord, Louisa still felt she could work best in Boston.

"Can't you write here, Lu?" Marmee asked wistfully.

Louisa was firm. Money was still needed for the Concord house. The doctor's bills for Beth's long illness must be paid. "I won't have the Alcotts always in debt if I can help it," she declared.

Back in her sky parlor, Louisa wrote furiously. Editors bought her tales and fantasies as fast as she could write them. She tried a more ambitious story for the *Atlantic Monthly*, the leading literary magazine of Boston. The story came back with a note from the editor: "Stick to your teaching, Miss Alcott. You can't write."

"I was crushed and wanted to run home to Marmee," Louisa told Fred. "But I didn't *stay* crushed. This time I'll take fate by the throat and shake a living out of her!"

7. "My Year of Good Luck..."

In 1860, Louisa wrote "This has been my year of good luck." She had sent more stories to the *Atlantic Monthly*. "Write of things you really know and feel," Father had advised her. "And write the best that is in you."

It was hard for Louisa to discipline her hasty style of writing. But one day she sent off a story called "A Modern Cinderella." It was a little tale based on the true life romance of her sister Nan and John. "There—that's the best I can do for now," she told herself.

A few weeks later Louisa opened an envelope from the *Atlantic* at Mrs. Reed's boarding house. Her story was accepted. When a check for $50 tumbled out, she gave a whoop of joy that startled the more sedate boarders at the breakfast table. One elderly gentleman held up his ear trumpet in alarm. "Eh — what's amiss?"

"Nothing amiss — only I am famous!" Louisa shouted reassuringly into the trumpet, leaving the gentleman blinking in further bewilderment.

She dashed off on a shopping spree, bought Marmee gloves and flannel petticoats, socks and ties for Father, a purse for Nan, and a Michelangelo print she had seen May admire. As an afterthought she bought a bonnet for herself.

"The fifty dollars was glorious, but the editor's kind letter and his request for more tales meant even more," Louisa wrote to Father.

Fired by new ambition Louisa began to write her first novel. She called it *Moods*. The title was from a quotation by Mr. Emerson: "Moods are like a string of beads." Some beads were bright, some dull. It was a story of marriage with a tragic ending. She lay awake nights thinking about her characters and planning new scenes.

A happy letter from Marmee told Louisa that Mr. Alcott had been made superintendent of the Concord schools. He had always been a gifted teacher, and the village children flocked to him eagerly. "They even follow him after school," Mrs. Alcott wrote. "A dozen or more, the smallest hanging on his coattails, escort him home."

Louisa was delighted. Later her father announced that the Concord schools would hold a spring festival. "We have cattle and flower shows," Mr. Alcott said. "Let us each year have a show of our children." He organized games and recitations and a Maypole dance.

Louisa wrote a poem for the occasion and went home to see "400 happy children follow Father as if he were the Pied Piper." She added: "The whole town liked it except a few old fogies who want things as they were in the ark."

Louisa came home to Concord again in May for Nan's wedding. Louisa and May were bridesmaids. They had made their dresses of

Quiet Nan shared family fun and troubles, too, with her lively sister Louisa.

pale gray and carried roses from the garden. Sunshine flooded the old house.

Louisa heard Uncle Samuel May ask, "Wilt thou take this man to be thy wedded husband?"

Nan's eyes were only for "her John" as she answered, "I will."

After the wedding the guests joined hands on the lawn and danced around the bride and groom. Mr. Emerson kissed the bride.

Nan and John settled in Chelsea, near Boston. Louisa called their little house *The Dovecote*. She sighed to Marmee, "Nan settles into marriage without ruffling a single feather. I never could! I'm too full of tempers and sharp corners to marry anyone."

"You aren't as fierce as you think, my Lu," Mrs. Alcott smiled. "When your turn comes you'll find that love smooths the sharp corners."

Louisa shook her head. "I'd rather stay single and paddle my own canoe."

More serious events for the country began in 1860. Abraham Lincoln was the newly elected President. The South, which believed in slavery, split from the North, which hated slavery. Civil war broke the country apart.

Like all Americans the Alcotts were deeply concerned. Mr. Alcott had always hated slavery. He hated war just as much. Louisa was less peaceful by nature. She sniffed gunsmoke like a battle horse. "I am thankful I have lived to see the war to end slavery," she said. "I wish I could march off with the soldiers to fight."

"Concord is boiling over with patriotism," Louisa wrote later. "Troops drill in the village square; children march about with fife and drums. Flags fly everywhere with a general spirit of do or die."

Louisa rolled bandages and sewed for "the boys in blue" with other women. But she longed to do much more. She read an article by Dorothea Dix, who headed the army nursing corps: "After each battle hospitals are filled with wounded and dying, who lie without water or food because there is no one to tend them. We have few trained nurses. Volunteers are desperately needed. . . ."

Louisa drew out a sheet of paper. She hesitated a moment and took up her pen:

"My dear Miss Dix,
　　I am a woman in good health, earnestly
　　wishing to volunteer in the cause
　　of the Union Army.
　　I have always liked nursing. . . ."

A prompt acceptance came. Louisa would report to the Union Hotel Hospital in Georgetown, near Washington, D. C., as soon as possible.

Louisa's family took the news bravely. They knew the hardships and dangers of army nursing. Hospitals were crowded and filled with infection and disease. Nurses worked long hours with little rest and wretched food. But Father understood Louisa's call to duty. Marmee looked at her tall daughter and saw the determined set of her chin. "Go, my Lu, and bless you," she said.

"We had all been full of courage until the last moment came," Louisa wrote. "Then we all broke down."

8. "Nurse Lu May Die…"

After two days and nights of struggling with delayed trains and wartime crowds, Louisa reached the Union Hotel Hospital "too tired to feel excited, sorry, or glad," she wrote.

The dark old building looked more like a prison than a hospital. Louisa was given an iron cot with a thin straw mattress. Her roommate was a pert, red-haired lass who looked more like a schoolgirl than a war nurse. She gave Louisa a weary smile. "Call me Pinky. Everyone does. Supper's ready now. Come along and be

At the Union Hotel Hospital, Louisa jollied, coaxed, and tenderly nursed "her boys."

prepared for the worst." Louisa followed Pinky and faced her first army meal of stale bread and bitter tea. Pinky introduced Louisa to the other nurses. "The matron will take you to your ward tomorrow and teach you what to do," she told Louisa.

There was little time for teaching next morning. Before Louisa could meet the men on her ward, ambulance wagons rattled up to the hospital door with wounded from the bloody battle of Fredericksburg. Doctors and nurses were called on emergency duty.

Louisa was bewildered with sudden orders.

Soldiers were carried in to lie on the floor. No one seemed to be in charge. Louisa ran wherever she was called. She fetched medicines and bandages and ladled hot soup for the exhausted men, pausing with a word for each. She was touched by the number who returned her smile or mumbled a hoarse "Thank ye, Nurse."

Toward dawn Louisa felt her bones melt with weariness. Then she looked up to see a woman in gray moving between the rows of stretchers.

"That's Miss Dix." Pinky nudged Louisa. "She always comes when they bring in more wounded."

Louisa stared curiously. She had expected Miss Dix to be a large, heroic figure. Instead she saw a woman who looked like a small, frail grandmother. Miss Dix moved briskly, counting stretchers, speaking to the doctors, checking supplies. When she looked at the soldiers, there was a deep sadness in her eyes.

Later Miss Dix spoke to Louisa. "I have read and admired your stories, Miss Alcott," she said.

"You are brave to volunteer. I'm sure you see how desperately we need you."

Louisa was soon the favorite nurse in her ward. The men liked her jolly, friendly way and called her "Nurse Lu." Louisa wrote home:

"Up at six, dress by gaslight, run through my ward and throw up windows, though the men grumble and shiver ... Poke up the fire and add blankets, joke, coax and command ... Till noon I trot, trot, giving out rations, cutting up food for helpless boys, washing faces, teaching my attendants how beds are made or floors are swept, dressing wounds, taking Dr. F. P.'s orders ... wishing all the time that he would be more gentle with my big babies. . . ."

A grizzled little Irishman who had lost a leg in battle was Louisa's devoted helper. His name was Tim O'Toole. He stumped through the

ward on crutches, pushing Louisa's cart of linen and medicines. The top of Tim's head barely reached Louisa's shoulder, but at least once a day he begged "Nurse Lu" to marry him. Louisa's refusals were as comical as Tim's proposals. The other patients were convulsed with laughter.

Taking her turn at night duty, Louisa watched over the sleeping ward. Under the shaded lamplight, she wrote letters home and filled pages in her journal.

On one midnight round Louisa walked past the beds. She paused beside a lad with pneumonia to tuck in a blanket and give him a sip of water. He whispered, "You are real motherly, ma'am."

She bent over a twelve-year-old wounded drummer lad. He was sleeping, but his pillow was wet with homesick tears.

Near the end of the row Louisa stopped beside another patient. He was John Sulie, a bearded young blacksmith with a chest wound. She heard him sigh.

"Are you in pain, John?" Louisa asked.

"Nothing I can't bear. Only I was wishing I could write a letter home."

Louisa brought pen and paper and copied down by candlelight the words John whispered to her. When she sealed the letter John sighed, "I feel better now."

The next day Pinky woke Louisa to say that John was worse. Louisa dressed and hurried to the ward. John stretched out both his hands.

"I knew you'd come! I guess I'm moving on, Ma'am," he whispered.

Louisa took his hands. They were rough and calloused from work, but gentle as a child's.

When John died Louisa went to her room and wept. Pinky patted her shoulder sympathetically.

Long hours of work weakened Louisa's health. Many of the nurses were sick. Some died of fevers. Louisa caught cold and developed a cough. The doctor ordered her to bed, but when Louisa learned there was no nurse to take her place, she shook her head. "I won't leave my boys," she said.

A few days later Louisa fainted. Pinky ran

for a doctor. Louisa heard voices through a haze of fever. "Typhoid," one said. "Pneumonia . . . very serious," said another. She was too ill to listen. For days she drifted through feverish dreams, calling for Marmee to bring her water.

The men in Louisa's ward were anxious when they heard she was ill. Tim O'Toole stumped off to ask the doctor how she was and came back with a long face. "Nurse Lu may die," he told the men. Gloom settled on the ward.

Miss Dix came to see Louisa and telegraphed Mr. Alcott: *Come at once.*

One morning Pinky called Louisa. "Wake up, Lu — see who's here."

Louisa opened her eyes to see Father bending over her, "like the dearest angel in a shabby overcoat," she wrote later.

"I've come to take you home, Lu," Mr. Alcott said.

Pinky packed Louisa's trunk. Miss Dix came to say good-bye at the train and brought a basket of fruit and medicines. "Miss Alcott, you have done as much for your country as any soldier,"

Miss Dix said. "I wish we had a thousand nurses like you."

As the train started Louisa looked out to see a group of her "boys in blue" on the platform. Every man from her ward who was able had come to see "Nurse Lu" off. They all saluted. Tim O'Toole waved a crutch.

Louisa's eyes blurred with tears. She waved back feebly.

At home Louisa grew worse. For weeks she was delirious with fever. Marmee and May nursed her, and she grew better slowly. One day she was able to sit up. She looked in a mirror. Her thin, big-eyed face seemed like a stranger. Her long dark hair had been cut off during the fever.

"My one beauty gone!" Louisa nearly wept. Then she laughed weakly. "At least they didn't cut off my head."

One evening the family had cheering news. Mr. Alcott came home from a lecture in Boston to announce, "Nan and John have a fine baby boy!"

Louisa and Marmee flung themselves on him with joyful questions. "How much does he weigh? What color hair? What will they name him?"

"What luck — a jolly little lad for our family of girls!" Louisa clapped her hands.

The next week Louisa had a bitter disappointment. All through her illness she had planned to go back to the hospital. Now the doctor shook his head. "You will not be strong enough to work again for many months, Miss Alcott." Louisa was miserable. She felt she had deserted the soldiers. At night she awoke thinking she heard "her boys" call.

Another evening Father came home from Boston with more good news. He had shown some of Louisa's letters from the hospital to the editor of *Commonwealth*, a newspaper.

"If Miss Alcott will get the letters ready, we will print them," the editor had said.

For the first time Louisa felt some of her old energy. She worked at her desk putting together her letters and the journal she had written in the hospital. She laughed as she remembered Tim O'Toole's comical proposals. She wept again over brave John Sulie. "If I can't go back to nurse my boys, at least I can write about them," she said to Marmee. "I can tell their families how brave and funny and tender soldiers can be."

Copies of the paper with Louisa's articles sold out quickly. Later they were published in a book called *Hospital Sketches*. The books sold as fast as they could be printed.

Letters poured in to Louisa. "I pray some nurse as kind as you was with my son when he died," one woman wrote. A doctor wrote, "Thank you for writing of the soldiers' character, which we doctors were often too busy to see."

Father's praise meant most to Louisa. "You have written out of your experience and your own heart, and you have put true life into your book," he said.

9. "Will Laddie Do?..."

Encouraged by the success of *Hospital Sketches*, Louisa went back to work on her novel *Moods*. It was refused by several publishers. Meanwhile she wrote more magazine stories.

In 1865 the long War Between the States ended. North and South were united again; slavery was ended. Louisa celebrated thankfully with other Americans.

With business improving, publishers were looking for new books. One accepted Louisa's

Moods. The book sold well at first, and Louisa enjoyed being a "literary lioness." "A very small lioness," she wrote home modestly. "More like a tabby cat."

The next year Louisa was restless. "I feel stale," she told Fred Willis. "I wish some big change would stand me on my head and shake new ideas out of me."

The change came unexpectedly. A friend of Louisa's asked her to go to Europe as a companion to his invalid sister. Louisa had always dreamed of traveling. She seized the opportunity. Crossing the ocean she was filled with excitement, but she soon found traveling with an invalid difficult.

"I take every free moment to see the sights," Louisa wrote home. "I wander from palaces and cathedrals to back alleys and come back to give Miss W. tonic and pills and powders. I paste on a cheerful smile each morning and pray that it will stick until evening."

One November day the travelers reached Vevey, on Lake Geneva in Switzerland. They were shown their rooms, and Louisa flung open the window. The lake was like a clear blue mirror. Snow-covered mountains rose against the sky beyond, and late roses bloomed in the garden below. Paradise must have looked like this in *Pilgrim's Progress*, she thought.

Miss W. went to bed early, and Louisa went down to dinner, grateful for a free evening. Most of the hotel guests were elderly. A pompous retired officer with two washed-out looking daughters talked loudly about the poor manners and outlandish clothes of the younger generation.

Suddenly, from across the room, Louisa caught a glance from a pair of merry dark eyes. A young man raised his wine glass to her.

After dinner the tall young man bowed to Louisa. "We both laugh at the good gentleman who says young people do not have manners. Since we laugh together we should be friends. I am Ladislas Wisinewski. It is a Polish name. One does not *say* it as much as *sneeze* it. Like this—Ladislas Wis-in-*ewski!*"

"Ladislas Wis-in-*ewski*!" Louisa sneezed obediently. They both laughed.

Ladislas had an idea. "I can teach you French, while you teach me this beast of an English. Shall we begin tomorrow, after lunch—in a boat on the lake?"

The next afternoon Louisa held her breath until Miss W. settled for her rest. Then she raced for the dock and found the young man waiting with a boat. They rowed together in the golden sunshine.

"I can't keep sneezing each time I say Ladislas Wisinewski," Louisa said. "You must have a nickname. Will Laddie do?"

"Excellently," he smiled. He told Louisa he had fought in the revolution, when Poland tried to free herself from Russia. The revolution had failed, and he had been a prisoner of war and ill with "an affair in the chest." Now he had escaped to Switzerland.

Laddie was a musician. When he was well again he would go to Paris and open a studio to teach music.

Louisa listened as she had listened to other young soldiers when she was a nurse in the Army hospital. Laddie coughed badly and was pale and thin. "He is still sick," she thought. "He needs care and cheering up, and I shall give it to him if I can."

One evening Laddie played the piano in the hotel parlor. Louisa listened with the other guests. At the end he played the Polish national anthem and rose to look straight at Louisa. "To America," he said. "May the freedom she has won be ours also some day."

There was something warmer than patriotism in Laddie's dark eyes. Louisa felt herself blush. "I must remember that Laddie is years too young for me," she told herself.

The days flew by. Louisa was too happy to count them. She and Laddie took every free moment together. They packed picnic lunches and climbed the hills above the lake.

The day came for Louisa and Miss W. to leave for Nice, on the French Riviera. "I do not say good-bye — only *au revoir*," Laddie said. "I shall be in Paris by spring. We will meet somehow."

Six months later Louisa came to Paris unexpectedly. Miss W. had decided to stay in Nice, and Louisa was free. She wrote to Laddie and took a train for Paris. "Will Laddie have forgotten me?" she asked herself.

On a rainy evening Louisa stepped off the train in Paris. The big station was noisy. Suddenly a familiar cap waved.

"Hello, my Lu!"

"Hello, my Laddie," Louisa called back.

A minute later her hand was tucked under Laddie's arm. "Paris and I make you welcome," he said.

For two happy weeks they explored the city, their hearts as bright as the spring sunshine. Each face they saw seemed to smile at them.

Louisa was delighted to see that Laddie looked well again. "I am strong and I cough less," he said. "Already I translate an English book into Polish. Next month I begin teaching music."

On the last evening they walked along the river bank in the moonlight. "These weeks have

been like a happy dream," Louisa said. "Tomorrow we must wake up."

"Stay here, my Lu," Laddie said. "We can go on dreaming."

For a moment Louisa was tempted. Then she shook her head. "I'm too old for you, Laddie," she said. "I have a family to take care of in America. I have work to do."

They parted at the railway station. From the train window Louisa put out her hand for a last farewell. Laddie kissed it and a tear rolled down his cheek. The drop glistened on her glove long after Paris was out of sight.

Back in Concord Louisa hugged and kissed her family. Her young nephew Freddie greeted "Aunt Weedy" with shouts of welcome. Nan's youngest son John, a rosy-cheeked baby, sat on Louisa's lap.

Louisa looked around the circle of loving family faces. "I've been a million miles away. Now I'm home," she said.

The next morning Louisa stared at the pile of bills. "We owe the butcher, the grocer, the doctor, and May's art teacher," she exclaimed in despair. "Why didn't you write and tell me that you needed money?"

"We wanted you to be happy," Mrs. Alcott said.

Louisa hated debts. But she smiled at Marmee's anxious face. "Bless you, I *was* happy."

That night Louisa shut the small packet of Laddie's notes into a desk drawer and shut it firmly. Only her writing could pay the family bills. She uncorked the ink bottle. Then she bent her head over the blank paper and began a new story.

Editors were ready to buy Louisa's work. Still she could not write fast enough to earn the money needed. She took a room in Boston, as she still found it easier to write there. One day she read that *Frank Leslie's Monthly* offered a prize of $100 for the most exciting story of mystery and adventure. Louisa remembered the "blood and thunder" plots she had written as a child. Half in fun she dashed off a lurid tale called "Skeleton in the Closet."

A week later Louisa won the $100 prize.

Leslie's wanted more stories, the more thrilling the better. She wrote "Behind the Mask," "The Marble Woman," and "The Mysterious Key." Each brought another $100.

Not even Louisa's family knew she had written the stories, for she never signed her real name. Later she confessed the secret to her mother. "I don't like writing anything I'm ashamed to sign my name to," she said. "There's nothing really wicked about the stories. But they're badly written and full of trumped up thrills and horrors. I shan't write any more, now that the debts are paid off."

She ended with a sigh. "Deary me, ma'am — I wish you and Father hadn't brought us up to be so high-minded! Then I could earn a fortune writing trash and we could all live happily ever after!"

10. "Meg, Jo, Beth and Amy Were Us..."

One morning in 1867 Louisa talked to Thomas Niles, who was an editor in the Boston publishing company of Roberts Brothers.

Mr. Niles smiled. "Miss Alcott, I have suggested before that you might write a book for girls," he said. "Won't you consider it?"

Louisa frowned. "I'd rather write about boys, since I always played with them and knew them best. Besides, girls' stories nowadays are trashy sentimental tales, or else stuffed with dull and preachy morals."

"But if you write a book about girls who are lively and real, I believe it will sell," Mr. Niles said. "Why not try a few chapters and let me see them?"

Louisa was still doubtful. She went home to visit and told her mother what Mr. Niles had said. "The only girls I knew well were my own sisters. Writing about them would only be telling about our family and our games and fun and the hard times we had growing up," Louisa said.

Marmee agreed with Mr. Niles. "Write about growing up just as you remember it," she said. "Tell about the sad things that happened and the funny ones. If you write honestly, girls will enjoy reading about others who think and feel as they do."

Louisa stayed in Concord to begin the new book. "Perhaps it will help me remember the old days to see the old places," she wrote to Mr. Niles. She could look at the barn at *Hillside* where the Alcott girls had given plays and the old attic where the Pickwick Club had met.

Days passed; still Louisa did not begin the new book. Then one morning she sat at her desk. The memory of a long ago Christmas Eve drifted back. She imagined the fields white with snow and four sisters gathered before the fire. She printed a title on the first page:

LITTLE WOMEN

Chapter 1

"Christmas won't be Christmas without any presents," grumbled Jo, lying on the rug.

"It's so dreadful to be poor!" sighed Meg, looking down at her old dress.

"I don't think it's fair for some girls to have plenty of pretty things, and other girls nothing at all," added Amy with an injured sniff.

"We've got Father and Mother and each other," said Beth contentedly from her corner. . . ."

Scene after scene came back to Louisa as she worked. She was writing about her own family,

Meg, Jo, Amy, and Beth gather around Marmee
in this illustration from *Little Women*.

but she gave her characters different names. In the book she called the Alcotts the March family. Mr. and Mrs. March were Father and Mother. Meg, the oldest daughter, was Louisa's sister Nan. Amy, the youngest, was May. Only Beth kept her true name. Jo, the second daughter, was Louisa herself, with her temper and her tomboy ways and all her topsy-turvy feelings. Jo's ambitions and struggles as a young writer were Louisa's own.

Some of the other characters in *Little Women* were mixtures of real people Louisa had known. Mr. Laurence, the stern, kind, next-door neighbor, was partly Mr. Emerson and partly Louisa's Grandfather May.

When Louisa wrote about Mr. Laurence's grandson Laurie, she was remembering Fred Willis, who had been a jolly, teasing brother when the Alcott girls were young. In the later romantic part of the story, Laurie was more like Louisa's young Polish soldier Laddie in Vevey and Paris.

"I still can't believe girls will be interested in

a book that has no exciting plot," Louisa told her mother. "I'm only telling the story of a family. The Marches struggle with being poor just as we did—and the four sisters have the same hopes and dreams and fun and disappointments we had."

Louisa finished the book in Boston and sent it to Mr. Niles. When his letter came Louisa tore open the envelope. At first Mr. Niles had not thought the story exciting enough, he wrote. But he had given it to his young nieces to read. "They beg for more about Meg, Jo, Beth, and Amy! If other young girls are as enthusiastic, *Little Women* is a sure success!"

The book was rushed to the printers, to be ready for the Christmas sales. Orders came in by the thousands. "Every girl in America expects a copy of *Little Women* under her Christmas tree," Mr. Niles told Louisa, beaming.

After years of struggling Louisa was dizzy with such sudden success. "I am 36 years old," she said. "But I feel as though I were just born!"

When the first big payment of royalties for

Little Women was paid, Louisa took the money
to Concord. She found the family gathered at
supper. May was at home. Nan and John and the
little boys were visiting.

Louisa put the royalty check in Marmee's lap.
"A little surprise," she said.

There was a stunned silence as the others
peeked at the check. In all their lives the Alcotts
had never had such riches. Then the joyful
exclamations broke forth. "What shall we buy

first?" "A silk dress for Marmee!" "Books for Father!" "Pastels for May!" "Jackets for the boys!"

"No! A toy train — *please* Aunt Weedy?" Freddie and Johnnie begged.

"Why, bless me, I'm a rich relative!" Louisa exclaimed. She held out her arms. "You shall have all you want!"

In Boston again Louisa found herself famous. Her book had been written for girls, but the characters were real and the writing so lively that people of all ages were reading *Little Women*. When critics praised her work Louisa was modest. "I didn't make up the book," she said. "We lived it. Meg, Jo, Beth, and Amy were *us*!"

Mr. Alcott was proud of Louisa's success. He wrote home from a lecture tour, "I am introduced everywhere as the father of *Little Women*."

Sacks of mail brought letters from Louisa's young readers. They loved all the March sisters but especially Jo. Louisa had made Jo, with her lively tomboy ways and her mixture of good and

A GIFT BOOK FOR THE FAMILY

LITTLE WOMEN.

ILLUSTRATED.

This, the most famous of all the famous books by Miss ALCOTT, is now presented in an illustrated edition, with

Nearly Two Hundred Character-istic Designs,

drawn and engraved expressly for this work. It is safe to say that there are not many homes which have not been made happier through the healthy influence of this celebrated book, which can now be had in a fit dress for the centre table of the domestic fireside.

One handsome small quarto volume, bound in cloth, with emblematic cover designs. Price $2.50.

ROBERTS BROTHERS,
Publishers, Boston.

This advertisement for *Little Women* shows the March girls acting out *Pilgrim's Progress*.

bad and her joys and troubles, such a true-to-life character that every reader felt as if she were reading about herself. "Please write more and tell who Meg, Jo, Beth, and Amy marry," the letters begged.

Mr. Niles wanted a second part to *Little Women* as soon as possible.

Louisa took up her pen again. Often she wrote late at night. Mrs. Reed worried about her health.

"My publishers are in a hurry," Louisa explained. "I must finish the second part of the March family story, or my young readers will perish of curiosity. But I won't have Jo marry Laurie to please *anyone*!"

The new volume of *Little Women* began with Meg's wedding to John Brooke. Louisa described it exactly as Nan's wedding to John Pratt had been. She wrote of Beth's illness and death and of her own love and grief.

In the book Laurie fell in love with Jo and begged her to marry him, but she refused. Later Laurie married Amy, the youngest sister.

In the last chapters Jo married Professor Bhaer. Louisa did not describe him as either young or handsome, but as a big, shy man with a curly brown beard and the kindest, twinkling blue eyes. The Professor was an imaginary character. Some readers thought he was like the distinguished Professor Rimmer, who had been May's art teacher. But perhaps Louisa was also remembering the big, gentle blacksmith, John Sulie, she had nursed in the army hospital.

The second part of *Little Women* was as popular as the first. It was soon translated into German, Dutch, and French. All over the world girls laughed and wept over Meg, Jo, Beth, and Amy.

Money from royalties poured in to Louisa. "Dreams come true every day," she exclaimed. "May can study abroad and be another Michelangelo. Marmee can sit by the fire and have a dozen flannel petticoats to keep her cozy. Father shall have all the books he wants!"

It did not occur to Louisa that her dearest wishes were seldom for herself.

11. "My Promise Kept..."

After *Little Women* everything Louisa May Alcott wrote was a success. She paid every family debt. "I used to think that if ever I were rich and famous I'd sit down and rest," Louisa said to May. "But magazine editors ask me for stories and articles. Mr. Niles wants a new book for Christmas sales. There are more family expenses. So I keep pegging away."

Louisa's new book was called *An Old Fashioned Girl*. The heroine was a girl named Polly, who

Louisa's "nevvys," Freddie and Johnnie, were always ready for a romp with Aunt Weedy.

came from a wholesome country family background. The story told of Polly suddenly plunged into city life. Louisa wrote her own dislike of fashionable society ways through Polly's honest, fun-loving character.

One October afternoon Louisa put down her work and traveled out to her sister Nan's house in Chelsea. "I've written all day. My head is empty as a coconut. You could rattle it," Louisa told her sister. "Please may I borrow two boys for a game of tag?"

Young Freddie and Johnnie greeted their favorite author-auntie joyfully. Ten minutes later Louisa was racing through the yard. She tagged Freddie first and made a lunge for Johnnie's shirttail.

When Nan called them in for supper she eyed Louisa's muddy shoes and torn skirt. "I must say you don't look much like Miss L. M. Alcott, the famous authoress."

"Oh, bother being famous if it means giving up fun!" Louisa piled up her hair and jabbed in two pins to hold it. "I've always wanted boys to romp with. Now you've given me a pair of nevvys, and I mean to enjoy 'em. Besides, how can I write for children if I don't have some to play with?"

Later that evening Louisa worked at her desk. The fresh country air had blown out of her brain, and her head ached.

When her headaches grew worse Louisa went to see a doctor. "You have worked too hard, Miss Alcott," he said. "Take a holiday."

Louisa would not stop until *An Old Fashioned Girl* was ready to publish. "Perhaps I can take a holiday now," she said. "May is longing to study the art masterpieces in Paris and Rome. We could go traveling."

Louisa and May sailed for Europe in 1870 with a friend, Miss Alice Bartlett.

The trip was very different from Louisa's first voyage abroad. Instead of being tied to a fretful invalid, she and her companions were free to wander as they wished. "We rest and

May sent home a sketch of the weary travelers in their sitting room in France.

gaze at the sights and laugh a great deal," Louisa wrote from France. "My *parlez-vous* is no better than ever, but May speaks French prettily, and Alice can rattle off German and Italian. I follow in their cultured footsteps, mumble a few syllables, and smile graciously."

On a late summer day they stopped at the little hotel in Vevey where Louisa had met Laddie. Louisa stood at her open window. A soft moon shone over the lake where she and Laddie had rowed. She could almost hear the dip and splash of their oars and the echo of their laughter.

She wondered whether Laddie knew she had written about him as Laurie in *Little Women* or whether he had ever heard of the book.

The travelers came to Rome. There a letter waited with sad news from the Alcott family. Nan's husband, John Pratt, had died suddenly. Louisa and May were grief-stricken. "Dear Nan has lost the kindest, best husband in the world, and we have lost the dearest brother," Louisa wrote home.

A few mornings later May was surprised to find Louisa working at her desk before breakfast. Louisa had started a new book. "I'll call it *Little Men,*" she told May. "I woke up this morning with a whole plot in my head." She went on writing as she spoke. "Nan will need extra money to take care of herself and the boys without dear John. I must write a new book to help them."

In *Little Men* Louisa carried on the story of the March family. Jo and her husband, Professor Bhaer, began a school for boys in their big house, *Plumfield.* They raised two healthy, merry children of their own. Many boys in the school were troubled or lonely. Professor Bhaer gave them special teaching, and Jo's cheerful, motherly care made the lads feel at home.

Louisa had always wished for a household of noisy, mischievous boys. She wrote about the Plumfield boys as if they were her own, and put much of her father's philosophy of teaching into Professor Bhaer's patient understanding of his young pupils.

Young Rob and adventurous Nan have lost their
way in this illustration from *Little Men*.

There were scenes of jolly family fun — picnics and holidays and weekly pillow fights.

One special boy, Nat, was Louisa's favorite character. He was the "bad" boy who ran away from school and came back still rebellious and unhappy. Louisa had often felt herself the only "wicked" person in her family. She wrote understandingly of Nat's troubles and worries and his struggles to be "good."

Day after day Louisa wrote while May visited art galleries and sketched the ruins of Rome. She sent the manuscript to Mr. Niles before she sailed for America, leaving May in England.

Little Men was published the week Louisa came home. Fifty thousand copies had already been sold. "It is another Alcott success," Mr. Niles told Louisa, as she settled down in Boston.

While Louisa had been writing her stories for children, her father had written books about philosophy and teaching that brought praise from scholars. He went on annual lecture trips to the West, and the tours were more successful each year.

While he was away lecturing, Louisa had bad news from Concord. Marmee was ill. Louisa went home at once and took charge of the house and nursing her mother. She sent for May to come home and help.

"Mother is to be cosey if money can do it," Louisa wrote in her journal later. "She seems to be now, and my long-cherished dream has come true; for she sits in a pleasant room with no work, no care, no poverty to worry, but peace and comfort all about her, and children glad and able to stand between trouble and her."

Although Marmee grew stronger, she was never really well again. Louisa spent her summers in Concord and her winters in Boston writing. She wrote two new books, *Eight Cousins* and *Rose in Bloom*.

The heroine of both books, Rose, was a girl growing up with eight boy cousins. Louisa described their early days of fun, then the troubles and moods of growing up. Rose says: "I've been gay, then sad, then busy, and now I'm simply waiting for what is to come next."

Money from the books continued to flow in. Louisa sent May back to her art studies in Europe, first in 1873 and then again three years later. May's paintings were being praised by the best art critics. "You should have your chance to go on with your career," Louisa told May.

The family saw May off gaily on a September day in 1876. "We were proud of our youngest, prettiest Alcott," Louisa wrote.

Letters from May came back to the family at home telling of her work. One letter began, "Joy! Joy! My painting is to be hung in the Paris Salon!" Two of her other paintings won prizes. But when May learned that her mother was ill again, she wrote anxiously to Louisa. "Shall I come home?"

"No," Louisa answered. "Marmee is proud of your success. Stay and work."

Nan was living in Concord now. Louisa had helped her buy the old Thoreau house. "It is a comfort to have Nan and the lively boys near," Louisa wrote to May.

Each month Marmee became weaker. Nan

came every day to help nurse her, and Louisa and her father watched at night. Sitting by Marmee's bed in the shaded lamplight, Louisa began a new book, *Under the Lilacs*. It was a gay story of a young boy and his trained poodle, Sancho, who traveled with a circus. Louisa wrote each night while Marmee's life faded away.

Abba Alcott died in November of 1877. "She smiled at us," Louisa wrote, "and whispered, 'A smile is as good as a prayer.' Then she said to Father, 'You are laying a very soft pillow for me to go to sleep on,' and was gone." She was buried beside Beth in the Concord cemetery.

Long ago Louisa had promised that Marmee should end her days in comfort. "Now I can rest —my promise kept," Louisa said.

Louisa's success went on. Thousands of loyal readers welcomed *Under the Lilacs*. But Louisa and her father were lonely in Concord. "Without Marmee, home has lost its soul," Louisa said. She left *Orchard House* and moved to Boston where she kept busy writing. Mr. Alcott was off on another lecture tour.

Ben with his circus poodle in an illustration from
Under the Lilacs

They looked forward to visits to Nan and the boys in Concord. Fred and Johnnie were sixteen and thirteen. "The lively lads keep Father and me from sinking into old age," Louisa wrote to May in London. "Fred is off to school in Boston. Not handsome yet but he will be. Meanwhile Father stuffs young John with lessons on science and philosophy till I wonder his head doesn't explode . . . Write us more of your happy doings. We love to hear of our 'little Raphael.'"

May's reply brought exciting news: she was engaged to a young Swiss, Ernest Nieriker. They would be married in London.

The family rejoiced. "You should go to London for the wedding, Lu," Nan said.

"I wish I could," Louisa sighed. "But I've promised a new book to Mr. Niles and stories to a dozen magazines."

She did not add the real reason. Headaches were troubling her again.

"You must have more rest," her doctor said. But Louisa went on working.

May wrote home of her wedding and of her

husband and their happiness in Switzerland.

The next year Louisa visited Nan in Concord and plunged into writing a new book, *Jack and Jill*. It was the story of a boy and girl hurt in a coasting accident. Louisa made the boy, Jack Minot, very much like her nephew Fred. She wrote of bright, mischievous Jill Pecq, remembering the little invalid girl she had tutored years before in Boston. The scene was Concord, and she wrote of the fun of village picnics and hayrides and May Day festivals.

Concord boys and girls heard of the book. Many stopped Louisa in the street and begged, "Miss Alcott, put *me* in your book."

"You shall *all* be in it," Louisa promised generously. She wrote chapter after chapter. "I shall finish soon," she wrote to Mr. Niles. But one day Nan found her ill with a violent headache. "You've worked too long and hard, Lu," Nan said anxiously. "You've given us all we need. Surely you can rest now."

Louisa shook her head. "I never learned how to rest."

May sketched her quaint bedroom in Paris and sent the drawing to her family.

Before *Jack and Jill* was published May wrote that she was expecting a baby, begging Louisa to come. Louisa had her steamship reservation, but when the time came, she was too ill to travel. She was bitterly disappointed.

May's baby was born in November. Her name was Louisa May Nieriker. Louisa wrote happily, "Another November birthday to join Father's and mine!"

Louisa spent Christmas with Nan and her

boys. Mr. Alcott came home from a lecture trip, and the Emersons called on Christmas Day. It was a happy family reunion.

A few days later Louisa walked to the village to mail letters and came home to find Mr. Emerson standing alone in Nan's parlor. He turned, his face stricken with grief, and held out his arms to Louisa.

"My child, I wish I could prepare you," Mr. Emerson said. "But alas, alas," His voice broke and he handed her a telegram. May was dead of a sudden fever after her baby's birth. May's husband had telegraphed, asking Mr. Emerson to tell her family.

A wave of grief swept over Louisa. "May was so young—so happy and successful. Now our pretty girl is dead." She put her head against Mr. Emerson's broad shoulder and wept.

May had left two messages. One said, "If I die, don't mourn; I have had much happiness in this short time." Her second message was for Louisa: She left her baby girl for Louisa to bring up as her own daughter.

12. "Young People
Make Me Young Again..."

"I am to be a mother for the first time at nearly fifty," Louisa wrote Mrs. Mary Mapes Dodge. "I buy nursery furniture and toys for my little daughter and pray I am not too old to be a good 'Marmee.'"

Mrs. Mapes was the editor of *St. Nicholas*, a children's magazine for which Louisa wrote many stories. She had become Louisa's close friend. When the baby arrived from Europe, Louisa wrote to Mrs. Mapes again: "Her aunt, Miss Nieriker, brought small Louisa May. I knew the baby at once. She has May's blue eyes and golden hair and May's own warm smile. We call her 'Lulu.' Father already adores his first granddaughter and plans her first lessons, though the mite is less than a year old! I am her devoted (though often weary) 'Aunt Weedy'... Pray do not expect any stories from me soon. For now my writing takes second place to my baby."

By the time Lulu was two years old, a nursemaid took care of her daytimes while Louisa worked. "My happiest hour is storytelling in the evening," Louisa wrote. "Lulu loves lambs and piggies and 'tats' and 'tittens,' and I make up tales to please her."

When Lulu was older Louisa made up a book of stories called *Lulu's Library*.

Lulu soon learned that she must play quietly while "Aunt Weedy" worked. One morning Lulu played with her paper dolls while Louisa answered mail from her readers. One letter was from a boy on a lonely ranch. He wrote that he had read *Little Men* six times, and liked the pillow fight scenes best. A young girl wrote that reading *Hospital Sketches* made her decide to be a nurse. Another asked, "Are the boys and girls in *Jack and Jill* real people?"

Louisa paused over a penciled letter from a woman who wrote that she had no money to buy her two children Christmas presents. Could Miss Alcott help? Louisa stood up. "Come, Lulu," she called. "You and I are going to buy presents for children we have never seen. We'll play Santa Claus."

Mr. Alcott called on Lulu and Louisa often. In his eightieth year Bronson Alcott had come into his greatest success. He wrote poems, and many were published in the best magazines. A new teaching center in Boston was named Alcott House in his honor. His lectures were more popular than ever.

Louisa and Nan were delighted to see their father enjoy the success that had been so long coming. They remembered the years he had worked at farming and chopping wood because no one would hire him to teach.

Mr. Alcott's greatest happiness was starting

Bronson Alcott at the entrance of his School of Philosophy, a dream come true.

his own School of Philosophy in Concord. Louisa wrote Mrs. Mapes, "For eight weeks in summer, some four hundred learned philosophers gather around Father and discuss the universe in gloomy terms. Nan and I bask in Father's glory and see that the multitude is fed!"

In 1882 Mr. Emerson died, and the Alcotts grieved for their oldest and best-loved friend. Another change came in the following year: Bronson Alcott suffered a stroke and became paralyzed. Louisa and Nan took care of him. "Anxious days, little hope," Louisa wrote. "Fifty lectures last summer were too much for Father at eighty-three. Still we remember how happy he was. . . ."

The strain of nursing her father and caring for Lulu was too much for Louisa. Her health broke.

"This time you *must* rest," her doctor ordered.

Louisa hired nurses to take care of her father. She found a cottage by the sea at Nonquit, near Boston, where she could rest and three-year-old Lulu could play on the shore. Lulu loved running in and out of the waves. "The water chases me, Aunt Weedy," she said.

"Quiet days and fresh sea air bring back my strength," Louisa wrote. "Fred and Johnnie come to visit." She added, "Young people make me young again."

When Louisa was well enough to work again, her publisher wanted a new volume of *Lulu's Library*. For years Louisa's readers had begged for another book about the March family of

Little Women. She had worked on *Jo's Boys* off and on, and now she was determined to finish it. The book told more of Jo and Professor Bhaer, and what the boys at Plumfield School did as they grew up.

Louisa was still not strong. Some days she could write only a few lines. But she went on working.

Young readers wrote begging for a picture of their favorite author, Louisa May Alcott.

Jo's Boys was finished at last in 1886. Louisa ended the book with the words, ". . . let the music stop, the lights die out, and the curtain fall forever on the March family." She put down her pen and sighed.

Tired as she was, Louisa did not give up the hope of writing more. "Plots and ideas buzz through my head like bees," she said. She looked forward to the time when Lulu would be older and her responsibility to her invalid father ended. "Then I shall burst forth with a dozen novels — see if I don't!"

One afternoon a young newspaper reporter came to interview Louisa.

"How did you start writing?" he asked.

Louisa laughed. "By making up ghost stories and frightening my sisters out of their wits with awful tales."

"Did you ever have a special place to write?"

"I never needed one. A pen and paper on my knee would always do. . . ."

"Have you any advice for young writers, Miss Alcott?"

"Only to write the best they can, to make the reader feel and care and laugh," Louisa said. "The strongest, simplest words are best. Work for twenty years—then they may find a style of their own."

In 1887 Louisa wrote: "We celebrated three November birthdays together. Father's and mine and Lulu's. Eighty-eight, fifty-five and eight years old. Lulu was enchanted with her dollhouse and a shelf of new books. Father and I received gifts and letters and flowers. I did not mean to cry today, but can't help it. Everybody is so good."

In March Mr. Alcott was suddenly worse. Louisa went to Concord to see him, forgetting to take a coat in her haste. She held his hand and spoke to him of long-ago days. They were both comforted. But on her way home Louisa shivered in the raw wind. That night she had a chill and then fever. The doctor was called. He feared Louisa might have pneumonia.

Bronson Alcott died the next morning. When the news came, Louisa was too ill to be told. Lulu went home with Auntie Nan. Two days later, on March 6, Louisa died. Father and daughter were buried on the Concord cemetery hill beside Marmee and Beth.

Near the quiet graves birds sing and wild flowers bloom each spring. Below the hill in Concord, *Hillside* and *Orchard House*, where the Alcotts lived, may still be seen.

Clothes and manners have changed since the days of Meg, Jo, Beth, and Amy. But their trials and joys and sorrows still live, for Louisa May Alcott's books speak to young hearts which never change.

Index